÷

Into Light

÷

Into Light

Poems and Incantations

Maja Trochimczyk

Copyright Notice

The Library of Congress Publication Data:
Trochimczyk, Maja, 1957–
    [Poems. English.]
    Into Light: Poems and Incantations /
    Maja Trochimczyk, author

Second Color Edition. 82 pages (xii pp. + 70 pp.);6 in x 9in.
Written in English. Includes 29 illustrations and one portrait.

ISBN 978-0-9963981-8-3 (paperback)
ISBN 978-0-9963981-9-0 (ePub format)
ISBN 978-1-945938-03-0 (color paperback)
 I. Trochimczyk, Maja, 1957–Poetry. II. Title.

10 9 8 7 6 5 4 3 2 1

Table of Contents

Poems ÷ 1

Incantations ⁓ 49

⁓

Introduction

After writing and editing a variety of books on music, dance, and poetry, and publishing poetry in various journals, I decided it is time to do something completely altruistic, without any shadows within, with a clear direction upwards, to the light. I pulled together my "enlightened" poems from the past 20yearsand created my own "incantations" — personal meditations and prayers, designed for quiet reading alone to uplift the soul in the morning, or provide a respite in a busy day.

My fascination with the twin themes of "Light" and "Love" dates back to my conversion period in Poland, when I first read the Bible from cover to cover and started collecting references to these mirrored themes. I thought of writing a mini-treatise on the topic of Divine Light to celebrate my baptism in 1987, when I became a Catholic at the age of 30. But somehow, I got too busy with other things and my planned treatise is now coming to life in an entirely different form.

This long and winding spiritual path was marked by a late start and guided by many unusual events, visions, and revelations —suitably so for a complete materialist, who would not believe in anything spiritual, unless personally experienced. I owe a debt of gratitude to those enlightened beings that have led me on the path of Light, and helped me discover the shortcut to Loving Kindness, the life of service.

First, my parents and grandparents taught me the joy of living close to Nature — planting and tending gardens; collecting bouquets of wildflowers and colorful leaves; picking berries and mushrooms in the forests; hiking; swimming; sailing; and gazing at the sky... They also introduced me to the world of Art — Music, Painting, Poetry, Film, Literature — and the world of Myth, of ancient Greece and the Native Peoples around the world, from Indonesia to the North Pole.

For my Father, Aleksy Trochimczyk, Nature and Culture were all that is (in many ways it still is all that is). Given the complexities of Culture and the imaginative layers of words, Nature has grown exponentially in its meaning and importance, since I first heard the skylark sing its heart out above a meadow in the spring and listened to the ringing silence in the fields at noon...

Somehow, this was not enough. Through a chance "synchronic" encounter, I met my Catholic Godmother, Sister Elia of the Franciscan Sisters in Warsaw, who taught me her rigorous "rules of conduct" as a perfect daughter, mother, student, and mystic — especially the Ten Commandments and the Two Commandments of Love. No matter how obedient to the Church, Sister Elia was not able to eradicate my interest in all things mystical, based on my personal experiences that were beyond her doctrine and my understanding. I took her name for my Confirmation, though – Elia, from Elijah, was a perfect choice I thought then, and I do now, listening to the breeze's gentle whisper...

Along the way, while making a discovery of a complete new continent of spiritual and religious writings, I read with great interest *The Cloud of Unknowing*, the writings and biographies of Blessed Hadewijch; Rumi; St. John of the Cross; Father Teilhard de Chardin; Thomas Merton; two twin souls, Discalced Carmelites Blessed Elizabeth of the Trinity (to be Canonized in October 2016); and Saint Thérèse of the Child Jesus from Lisieux, and many others, including poets Czesław Miłosz, Emily Dickinson, and the Beatles (*Yellow Submarine*).

One of the most influential books was the *Guidelines for Mystical Prayer* by English Carmelite, Ruth Burrows. The monastic tradition of mystic love, of seeking and discovering the Divine within one's heart has appealed to me much more than public and ritualistic aspects of Catholicism. I am appalled by the spectacularly vulgar opulence of the Vatican, and I do not believe Popes or Saints are to be worshipped. The Divine Light in every person's heart — yes. One, "infallible" man on a throne, claiming ownership of the world — certainly, not. I share this attitude with Giordano Bruno and many real, unknown saints.

And thus my journey continued. In the 2010s in California, I found insight and love in the poetry and friendship of the "Spiritual Quartet" – four women who have taken birds as their totem images while pursuing their own paths into Light, sometimes parallel, sometimes inter-woven. Lois P. Jones ("the Phoenix"), Susan Rogers ("the Hummingbird") and Ambika Talwar ("the Peacock") have been faithful companions and guides on my own way into the Awakening. I'm "the Dove" of love, they decided, and so I am.

The next stage of my spiritual discovery started with the end of life of my mother, Henryka Trochimczyk (neé Wajszczuk) who died on July 4, 2013. I decided to find out why she believed in reincarnation, had an amber pyramid on her bedside table, and talked to her house plants. The plants were extremely happy with her, but withered after she left, so that proved a shared emotional bond. Now I talk to my plants and they thrive...But reincarnation? Books by visionaries Edgar Cayce and Dolores Cannon have provided some answers. I realize now that my overall worldview has to be entirely reframed – time and time again, as I grow in understanding, kindness, and love.

Therefore, the poems and incantations in this volume are not Catholic *per se*. Since my search is not over, I do not express any particular approach to spirituality or religion, except for my own mystical focus on the unknown Source of us all, the Light that draws us near, the Love that keeps us alive and dwells in our hearts. Baptized as an adult into the Catholic Church, after a long search for the right path, I'm an usher in my local parish, and find enough light in the Scriptures to keep me nourished. Scriptures, not Catechism and dogma. I have experienced the revelation of cosmic unity, the brilliance of selfless love, the sweetness of gratitude, the relief of forgiveness, and the presence of light in everything— particles of air, grains of sand, leaves, rocks and clouds...

I seek enlightenment where it can be found. In addition to weekly Mass, I attend "light-giving" sessions at the Sukyo Mahikari Spiritual Development Centers (with Susan Rogers as my guide) and spiritual healing sessions given by inspired healers, filled with Divine Light and grace, Kimberly Meredith and Ambika Talwar.

Some of my "incantations" feature variations on Catholic prayers, the Shield of St. Patrick and Hail Mary. Other texts are variations on words borrowed from Kimberly Meredith, or

Messages by Archangel Michael channeled by Ronna that I found on YouTube, or stories about past lives that I would not have been able to accept as factual merely four years ago. I paraphrase ideas and inspirations from the *Convoluted Universe* books by hypnotherapist Dolores Cannon, *The Law of One*, the *Spiritual Development Course* by the Abbotts (Australia), and the *Emerald Tablets of Thoth.* If there are any others, whose ideas I may have adopted as mine without proper acknowledgement, Love and Light to you all!

There are many parallels and synchronicities in the mystical traditions. While reading the Prayer to Fukushima Waters, for healing of the environmental damage, written by Dr. Masaru Emoto, you might recognize the sections of the Catholic Mass: "Water, we are sorry" (*Mea Culpa*), "Water, please forgive us" (*Kyrie Eleison*), "Water, we thank you" (the Eucharist), "Water, we love you" (the Communion). At least, that's what it seems to me, but I've been an unusual sort of a Catholic, converted from a scientific-atheistic worldview, enriched by personal mystical visions, that lead to an immersion in Light and a communion with the One. The "divine indwelling" described by the Carmelites parallels the discovery of the Adamantine Particles of Light, the Sparks of the Divine Spirit and the loving connection to the Source contemplated in meditation, deep within the heart.

In addition to those already mentioned, I am deeply grateful for all my teachers and guides who showed me the way, either directly — by sharing with me their positive and inspiring ideas and actions — or indirectly — by doing things that were not positive neither in intention, nor in outcome, but still were able to teach me and guide me to the way into Light. Finding the way to becoming a Child of Light has been the greatest adventure of my life.

I leave my reflections to my readers, with the hope that they, too, follow their pathways into awakening, into the Light!

~ *Maja Trochimczyk* ~

Prior Publication Credits

Poems "A Passage," "Timelessness," "The Bluest," "A Subliminal Song," "The Gift of Patience," "In a Magnolia Courtyard," and "See, How we Dance?" appeared in art-themed chapbooks of Poets on Site, edited by Kathabela Wilson in 2008-2011.

Poems "Awakenings" and "See, How we Dance?" were published in a volume of poetry inspired by Susan Dobay's art, *On Awakening,* edited by Kathabela Wilson in 2011.

Poems "A Promise," "The Feast," "Of Bliss" and "Seeing Madonnas in a National Museum in Warsaw," were included in my chapbook for Sister Elia, *Glorias and Assorted Praises* (2007), while "Convergence" appeared in *Meditations on Divine Names* that I edited for Moonrise Press (2012).

"Rosa Mystica" was included in a chapbook on Beatrix edited by Kathi Stafford (2012) and repeatedly reprinted.

"The Cornerstone of the Soul" "A Lesson for My Daughter," and "Cosmos" were first published in the now defunct local monthly, *Voice of the Village*(Sunland, CA). These and other poems, such as "Repeat After Me," and "Meditation on Light" also appeared on my poetry blog, PoetryLaurels.blogspot.com.

÷

Into Light

÷

To my Children

May your Heart be light as a Feather
May your Smile be bright like the Sun
May your Days be sweetened by Laughter
Loving Kindness
and Fun

÷

Poems

"Over the Rainbow"

A Passage

a wild scramble through the rocks
scratched toes, bruised fingers, blisters

higher, faster, we can make it still
the golden glow is there
on the other side of the rift
in the curtains of stone
that slowly open
to reveal the glory
of a landscape
flooded by bliss,
a moment stolen
from time

higher

      faster

            we can

                  make it

                        still

A Walk in the Canyon

We walk on layers of
past lives. Fossilized shells
skin, bone, membrane.
Ripples in the sand
on the ocean floor
now frame the mountains.
The patterns sculpted
by waves linger on
after water disappeared.
Sand, sandstone, limestone.
Granulated, petrified by time.

falling– sinking – twisting – rising up

Like grains of sand
caught by the cosmic tide
we rise and fall with
the shifting clouds of light
and darkness. Words
change us into stone.
Words melt us in the fire
of compassion.

Like water, we flow
and disappear, droplets
of rain in the mountain stream

racing down the slopes
to the river, through the valley,
searching for the ocean.

The beating wings of the dove
struggle against the wind.

falling– sinking – twisting – rising up

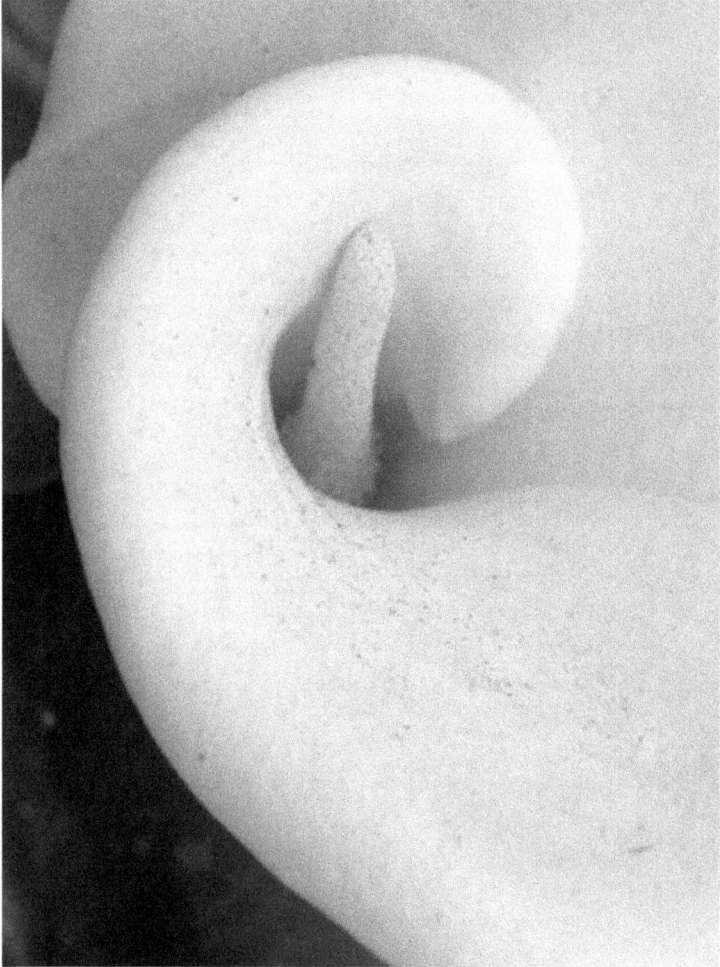

"Spiral into White"

No More

Slav, Sclave, Slave —
We are all one — under
That thumb of powers that be
Of powers that do not want us to be,
To become free, creative, enlightened

Slav, Sclave, Slave —
We are all one, united
In the will to connect, all one
In compassion, in awareness
Of the ground under our feet,
The warm soil, trees growing roots,
Sparkling clean water
Flowing to fill us.

Made of water and stardust,
We are all one under the sunrays
Reaching down to touch our skin,
Nourish our muscles.

We claim our freedom
To be wise —to be kind—
To carry each other's burdens
To stand tall, walk forward
Together —

NOTE: "Sclave" means "slave" in Latin; the name used by Romans for the "Barbarians" in the north-east of their empire.

Timelessness

Yes, there is time
Yes, there is weight
of the rocks on the skin
of the earth making
it harder to breathe
for the beast of eons

Yes, there are clouds
Yes, there is air
cut with wispy stripes
of whiteness wishing,
willing itself into being,
into solid forms that
dissolve in the merest
breeze, flee into nothing

Yes, there we are
Yes, matter stays
atoms, prions, electrons
dance in an endless cycle
of DNA spirals, molecules,
blades of grass and gravel

Yes, there is time to watch,
to catch the transient beauty
of living in red harmony
blood circling in our veins,
rock dust changing into stars

Awakenings

~ after a painting "City Whispers" by Susan Dobay

First to wake: the maple tree.
Up and up, sprouting from a seedling.
With a crown of burnished gold, white
diamond crystals for winter –
It slept through blizzards to flourish
dressed in pinks and celadons.

Second awake: the girl.
Watching the trees from her bed
Or her wheelchair. She cannot go far
Into the streets, filled with noise.
Protected by smooth glass panes
She sees the buds on each twig
Fill out until they burst
Into carmine, wrinkled bows
Small and shiny, maturing
As they change into the green.

The third: a robin calling out
To his friends, dispelling darkness
With his shrill fluted motives.
The spring is woven from his calls,
Warmed up in red feathers on his chest.
He came late to scratch the ground
For a worm to peck, a beetle.
The looping birdsong measures
The coming of days.
It floats up and up,
Above the rooftops.

The girl touches her curly blond hair
Growing longer, straighter

As the nurse braids it each morning.
The life, the light, she wishes
For this power to come in.
Make her walk, yes, make her walk.
She stretches up and up.

Outside, city whispers.

"City Whispers" by Susan Dobay

The Bluest

Oh, to float into blue distance —
a dream of weightlessness,
knowledge of nothing but the air
in the lungs, air carrying the limbs
from cloud to cloud into being,
into tranquility, into peace

All made of water, we live
in the Cloud of Unknowing
we breathe mist of a shroud
surrounding the mystical
peaks of the Ancient One
that will not be known
nor understood fully

We have to, we must fly
higher, we must grow wings,
strain in our childish hope
that we'll find the brilliance
hidden beyond the bluest
blue of infinity, of time

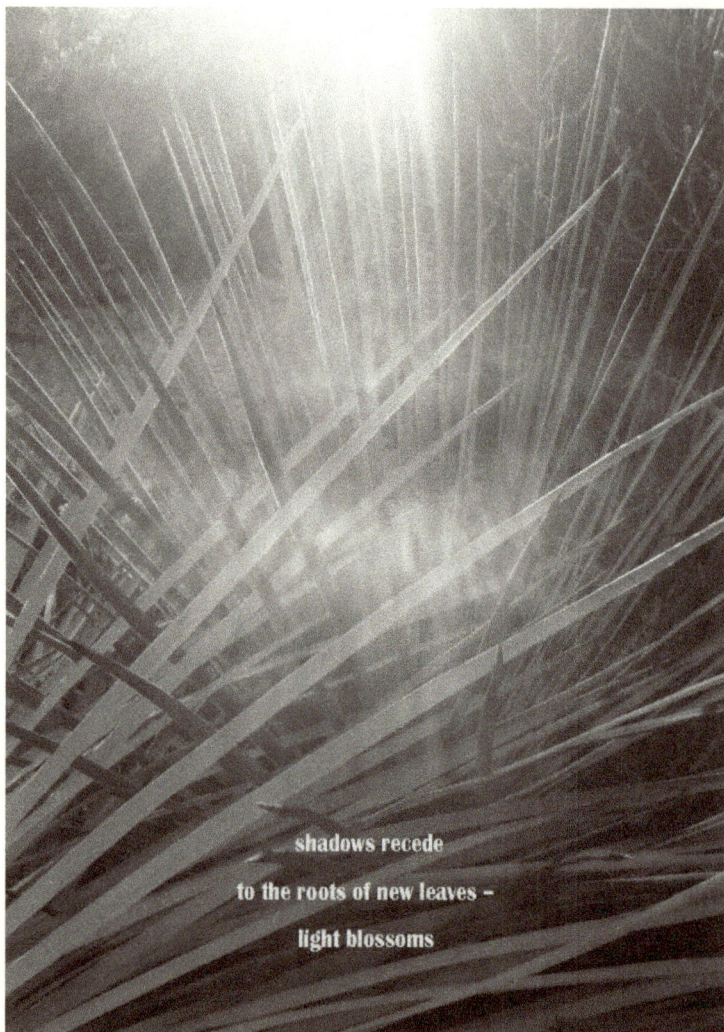

shadows recede
to the roots of new leaves —
light blossoms

A Subliminal Song

the yin and the yang
push and pull
dance and twirl
in the vortex of stars
interstellar dust
oscillates at the edge
of black holes before
imploding
into a new dimension
cosmos reborn
beyond limits
of disordered time

the yin and the yang
flow and recede
grow and wither
circulate in the blood
moving through
the veins, the heart
weaker, stronger
in tears and in smiles
falling into darkness
shining with wild flames
of boundless energy
new love, new life

The Way Out

If you feel darkness touching you,
its moving, sticky tendrils reaching out
to wrap around you, its magma
of opaque substance flowing slowly
to envelop and devour you —

Say: *No.*
Say: *Stop.*
Say: *Go away.*

Say:
I'm a sovereign citizen of the galaxy.
I invoke the law of free will.
I refuse to be touched by darkness.
I seek shelter in Divine Light.

Stand firm. Do not fall into the void
of fear, anger, selfish cruelty and hate.

Say:
I ask you kindly, my dark velvet beauty,
leave me, go where you belong,
where countless delights await you.
Do not fear Love. Do not fear Light.
Go find your peace. Go find your bliss.

See? The clouds are lifting. Black
cords disappear. Thank Light
for its brilliance. Thank Love
for its kindness. Thank Life
for its sweetest gifts
only you can find.

The Gift of Patience

squeeze your eyes tight
raise your face to the sun
see the magic kaleidoscope
of jagged shapes
under your eyelids

the white light heals
the white light erases
the white light sings
a new world into being
a world without torture
a world without shame
a new world

just close your eyes
just wait, do not peek
the grace will come
the grace will come
the white light sings

"White Ray"

Of Bliss

I'm burning but I'm not burnt
In agony, but not yet dying
Light streams out of my heart
Filled into overflowing
Sounds of an ancient tongue
Trigger a glimpse of a time
When the rose and the flame are one
Wreath of fire which engulfs me
Dissolving into stillness

A white wave reaches its destiny
The valley brightens
Under a shaft of sunlight
The air is sweetened with flutes
And harps —How obvious—
How delightful! A breath
of music cascades into silence

Love has no father, no mother
But this— Perfection
Of all things in all
Feelings collapsed into one
Not a longing, really
And not satisfaction.

Perfect fulfillment—
All dreams

Look Inside

There is a galaxy
twirling inside your chest.
Billions of multicolored suns.
Thick nebulae, droplets of planets
in azure and sage float through
the velvet darkness, spiral
in the waltz of the eons.

In this vortex, they dance,
they swirl, they sing. You are
their song — the resonant voice
of your galaxy, in harmony
with myriads of stars stretching
in all directions, beyond here,
beyond time, always now.

See, how the universe pulsates
with the divine love in its heart?

"Peace in Light"

The Feast

the fruit is ripe —
come and gather
the flowers are ready
for the taking —
come, enjoy

voices woven into tapestries
of sweet melodies, the violins'
harmonious chords
a rhythmic drumming
of the heartbeat
the dazzling multitude
of leaves and petals
rainbow geometry of life
air suffused with the scents
of lilac and jasmine
rich taste of honey
on your tongue
and the comforting warmth
of your beloved's hand

eat and drink
in lucid delight,
my dearest

the feast of Love
has begun

Seeing Madonnas
At the National Museum

Gothic Madonnas
with down-cast eyes
demurely
look within—

the infinity of love
spreads out
the galaxies of laughter
amidst nebulae of bliss

happy overabundance
marks their cheeks
with a half-smile
of knowing

Madonna of Krużlowa from the National Museum, Kraków

Rosa Mystica

The love that calms this heaven always offers welcome /
with such greetings to make the candle ready for its flame
~ Dante, Il Paradiso, Canto XXX: 52-54

I knew it all along (at least,
suspected)—— Beatrice's
swimming cap betrays
Heaven as nothing but
an oversized pool

where saints swim like fish
in the river of light
and God-Mother rests
on white lounge petals
of a Mystic Rose

Giovanni di Paolo's
illumined pages of *Il Paradiso*
unveil creature comforts
beyond the sapphire glow
of Dante's Empyrean

Angels curl in their pods
like babies asleep
on metallic wings
with round pillow halos
of shimmering gold

Multi-hued gowns of cobalt,
salmon, sage, and sienna
reveal the childish joy
of heavenly hosts
adoring the Trinity

Cherubs play hopscotch,
dance the *Sarabande*
twirl like a swarm of bees
among light-bursts that do not
sear their eyes with pain

Rushing waterfalls of laughter
sparkle in diamond waves
on the robes of our Mother
Daughter of her Son
figlia del tuo figlio

She gave Him a kiss
on the way to Rose Garden —
serene Love's Greeting
beneath seraphic wings

rainbows that cut our darkness

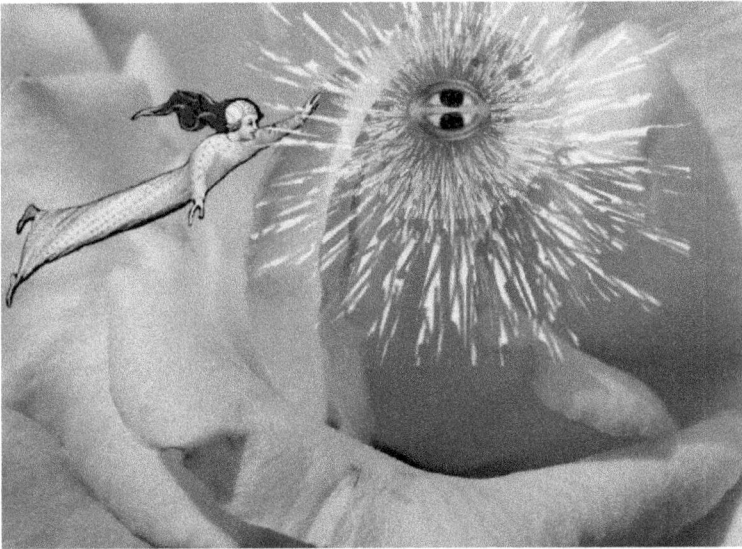

"A Collage with Beatrix," based on Giovanni di Paolo's illuminations
For Dante's *Il Paradiso*

A Lesson for My Daughter

After a ruby-colored glass of Merlot
I told my daughter
the secret of the Universe.

I solved it at noon, by the river.

Questions do not matter.

The right answer to life is: "Yes."

If you build a circle of "Yes" around you,
affirming the essence of beauty,
you'll be safe.

If you say "I love you" to everyone —
very quietly so they can't hear,
but you know —

You'll walk in a sphere of gladness
no insult or curse may pierce.

You'll be whole and holy—
living deeply where love blossoms,
laughter bubbles, and joy overflows.

The Cornerstone of the Soul

Fortitude:
Keep smiling. Grin and bear.

Justice:
Do what's right, what's fair.

Temperance:
Don't take more than your share.

Prudence:
Choose wisely. Show you care.

The Four Cardinal Virtues:
The cornerstone of the soul.

Once you've mastered the steps,
New ones appear —

Faith: You are not alone.
Hope: And all shall be well.
Love: Where we are.

"Amber Pyramid in Light"

How to Cross the Great White

We are almost there. The pink stretch
of light on the horizon.
The luminescent arch above
thick trunks, crowned with the lace
of twigs and branches. A gathering
of trees is calling us. Almost.

We have to cross the salty plain
without life — white, bone-quiet,
it stretches into the distance, pulls us
within — to forget, to linger, to remain
lonely, immobile, transfixed. Almost.

We look up to the ribbon of light
above the horizon. It shines
like a crystal egg of rose quartz,
the sign of solace, understanding.
We raise our gaze higher, to the aqua,
pearlescent, indigo firmament,
with trillions of stars watching us,
unblinking.

Each step takes us further, closer,
as we search for the contours
of Orion, his belt lost among
untold treasures.

Scattered nodules of light
sail through space,
sing the morning anthem.

The first birds stir in the branches,
comb their feathers,
wait for the awakening sun.

Eons pass. We walk
through the great absence.

Our steps echo
in the vaults of the Night.

"Hands in Light"

After the Crossing

Imagine Lethe, the river of forgetfulness
just behind you. Its foamy waves,
curling in darkness. You made it.
You did not forget. The Great White
Desert let you pass. It sighed heavily, unwilling.

You are here. Standing under the canopy
of stars in liquid amber sky. Your toes
sink into the carpet of evening grass,
the luxury of ermine smoothness.

You are sheltered by monumental trees,
weighing the ages with cosmic precision.
They remind you of the beak of the toucan,
its multi-colored feathers shining in the mist.

The path's unveiled — birds led you
all the way. You made it. You are here.
You remember. The verdant softness
beckons you to lie down, watch
the rainbow flight of the toucans,
the unfurling wings of dawn's
bright swans.

I'm glad you came. I'm glad we made it.
We are here. We did not forget.

The Vanishing Point

At the edge of an infinite ocean
That's breathing time into space
In the temple of light
Columns shine from within
With warm brightness
That comforts and heals

There are great halls and countless
Mirrors in this brilliant library of ages
Where you find all books, and all
Knowledge that was, is, and ever will be

In this temple of light
Where columns shine from within
We rest in the glow of wisdom
And learn who we are —
All one, all together, strands woven
Into a tapestry of thought and breath,
Undulating with life

It is done —we walk in
the door's open

"Holding a Lapis Universe"

See, How We Dance?

~ after Susan Dobay's "Musicscape 12"

Simon says — "grow"
and our roots reach for water
our branches for the sun

Simon says — "blossom"
and our pink petals open
in a gold mist of newness

Simon says — "sing"
and we let the breeze whisper
with hummingbirds, jewels, leaves

Simon says — "fly"
and we turn and turn again
in swirling clouds, voiceless music, dancing

Convergence

everyone is singing around me
everyone

awash in their voices
I stand in the Melbourne cathedral

English vespers, Communion
my heart races — I am still

I am taken— the white bread
becomes my body — I am the bread

white manna surrounding the world
in a blizzard — dancing, falling

I fly with the spirit-wind
encircling the globe

I multiply like loaves and fishes
in the desert

I am eaten, nourish millions
set them on fire

snowing manna
droplets of light

sparks of cosmic flames
everywhere

delighted by velocity
dizzying heights and depths

on terraced rice-paddies
in musty stone cathedrals

wooden churches
shining like amber at dusk

I'm the blanket of light
that covers the world

with serenity— ascending
in crystalline air— love sings

"Blessed by Light"

A Whale of a Song

They sing, as they ride the waves,
laughing. They sing to the depths
of the ocean, reaching its sandy bottom,
submerged peaks and valleys.

Their song echoes through
the crystalline expanse of the sky,
bounces off the translucent
rays of starlight.

They dance on the waves, weaving
the web of love from their song.

In the invisible rhythm of seven billion
heartbeats, they encircle the globe,
traversing all the oceans.

Did you know
that whales and dolphins
are our cosmic guardians?

Did you know
that Orca, the whale,
is my patron saint?

I have a totem stone to prove it,
a gift from a seer who once told me:

> *Do not forget to listen*
> *to life-giving music.*
> *Do not ever forget*
> *the song of the whales.*

From the Mountains

In flames,
smothered with charcoal
the mountains sing,
greening —
grass is their song
and sage and lily

resounding calm arising
from the slopes
shapes the air
into inverted bells

they call to me waiting
for my small voice
to dissolve
in their harmonies
and ring

like a blade of grass
stirred by the breeze
on the high meadow —
passing into silence

"My Whale Saint"

Cosmos

green rings around a red heart
sing in the darkness, sing
and blossom

light waves dance across
millions of years swirling
within black matter

the stars are born
the stars are born
radiance

green clouds around red suns
bloom in the vastness, bloom
filling the void

clusters of galaxies expand
crush and collide
the ages turn

before me — beyond me — through me

a spark of cosmic fire
I float up to the unknown
glow of the timeless "yes"

the stars are born
the stars are born
brightness

Gloria

it's so nice to be
glad
contentment knows no bounds
joy
grows from the fertile soil of
tears
spilled in a happiness that
love
only could bring back from the
lost
hours and evenings beyond
bliss
merging the end with the
start
in one magnificent moment

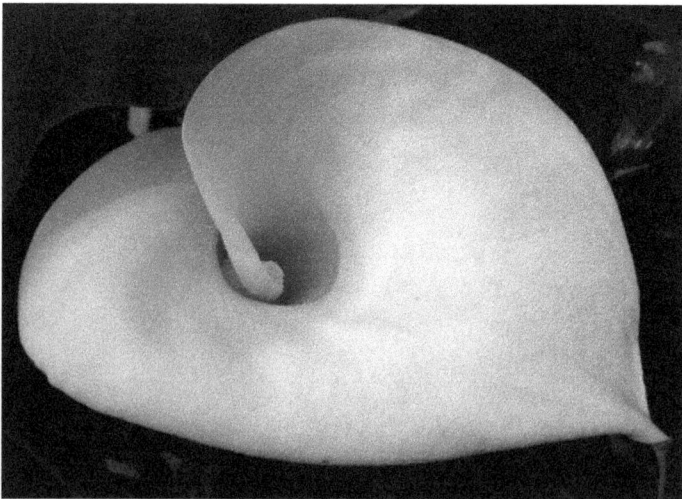

"A Pure Heart"

Elijah's End

And the curtains of fire open.
And God walks through.
And I fall on my knees
Struck down by the might
Of his presence.

And the ground under my feet
Roars and trembles.
And God is with me.

In awe, I do not dare to look
Into the laughing beauty of his eyes.
And the gale changes into a breeze.
And God speaks in a whisper,
Sweetly announcing
The end of the world as it was.

And the sun stops in its tracks.
And the world explodes.
Filled with love, so much love,
It could not bear existing
For one more minute.

— now it ends —
— now it blossoms —
— now it grows again —

A Perfect Universe

We live in a perfect universe
of what is, right next
to a galaxy of universes
of what could have been —
endlessly fascinating and desirable,
yet unnecessary.

A myriad of possibilities opens up
with every step, every gesture.

Choosing well —this is
"the narrow path."

"Walking into light"

On Squaring the Circle

It is a simple square that contains the circle —
four ideas, four words —

— *Sorry* — *Forgive* — *Thank* — *Love* —

No need for explanations,
long winding roads of words
leading into the arid desert
of heartless intellect, auras
of geometric shapes floating above
your head — a scattered halo
of squares, sharp-edged cubes
prickly triangles, and hexahedrons

No, not that. Instead let us find
the cornerstone. Simplicity.

Sorry — to erase the past

Forgive— to open a path into the future

Thank— to suffuse the way, each moment
with the velvet softness of gratitude

Love — to find a pearl unlike any other,
a jewel of lustrous shine — incomparable,
dazzling, smooth, pulsating sphere

A dot on the horizon grows
as you, step by step, come closer
until you enter into the shining
palace without rooms
where inside is outside,

the circumference is in the point,
the point in the circumference—

where movement is stillness
and stillness dances within —
traveling to a myriad planets,
suns, galaxies, with unheard-of
velocity, everywhere at once

Love everyone — Respect everything

*   *   *

So that's how you square a circle

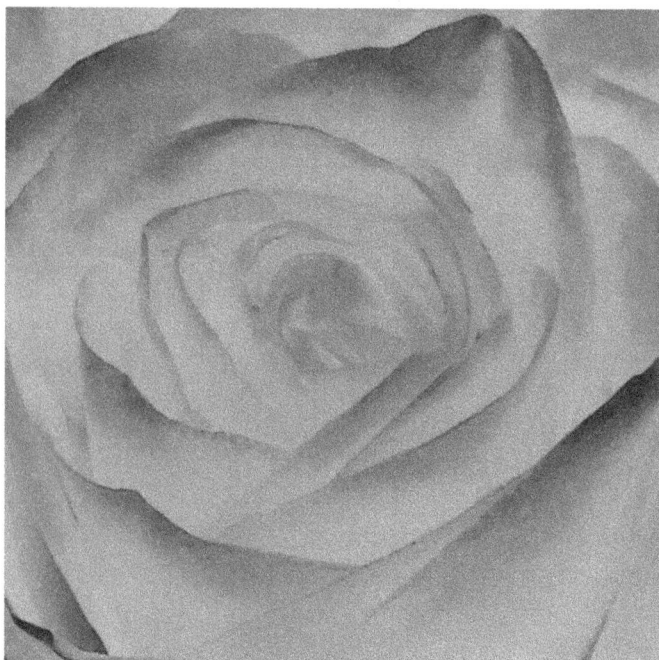

"The Nectar of Light"

Under the Midnight Sky

~ *for Ambika*

She said—*Close your eyes.*

You are in an opulent palace.
Look at the exquisite, velvet curtain.
What color is your curtain?

Open it, and step outside. Walk
through the colonnade of marble
to the garden beyond. It is night.

As you step onto the fresh, wet grass
you feel the coldness of the dew.
You look around. What do you see?

I look up at the brilliant darkness
of the midnight sky, veined with gold,
filled with constellations, marked

with the stripe of Milky Way
spilled by a startled goddess
across the spine of the Universe.

I see the fireflies of stars. My eyes
touch the light that left them
millions of years ago.

My mind stretches into infinity,
Touches star nebulae and swirls
in clouds of interstellar dust.

I see myself up there, the one star
that is linked to me, as we drift
further and further away.

The cord stretches and pulls me
up to the star, pulls me, with my star,
to where it all began, the One,

the heart of Love and Light,
the point and circumference,
the dot of singularity.

Star clusters grow inside me.
Galaxies flower within me, dancing
on their elastic, golden cords.

They converge and explode.
They escape and return, unbidden.
My mind maps the Cosmos.

My mind is the Cosmos.
Cosmos in my mind.
The Divine Mind.

In a Magnolia Courtyard

It is where you rest in the eternity
of pink magnolia happiness

while petals drop down
onto the pavement
in the open hands
of a Buddha sculpture
sharing your bench

where you wait
with magnolia teacups
for the rain nectar
to fill you with hope
after the parting
of clouds in the sky

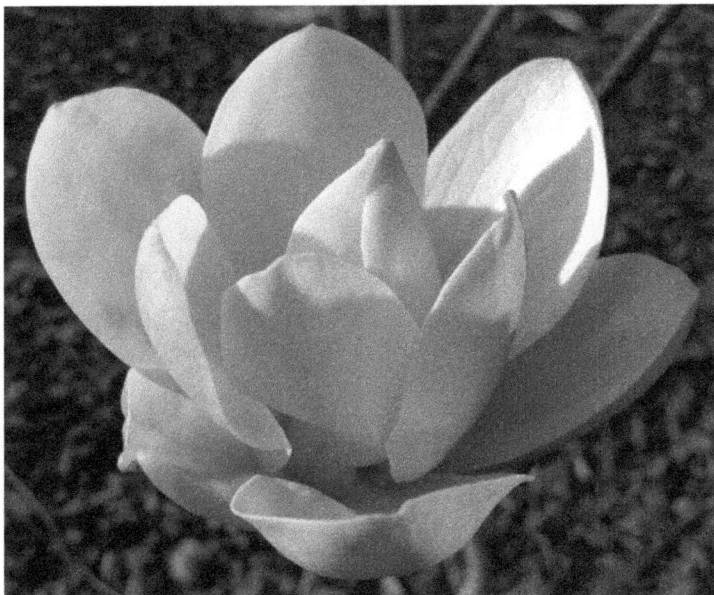

"Light Luxury"

Repeat After Me

After Prayer for Fukushima Waters by Dr. Masaru Emoto:
        Water, we are sorry /
        Water, please forgive us /
        Water, we thank you /
        Water, we love you

Yes, you can find it. /Your way out./
It is so simple. /First you say:/

I AM SORRY / – WE ARE SO SORRY./

We are the guilty ones,/ we are all at fault!

What happens next? /The door opens./
We stop at the threshold and say:/

PLEASE FORGIVE ME, / I FORGIVE YOU./

Forgiveness erases /all my fears,/
all our sorrows / The burden
of dead thoughts is lifted./ See?/

We float up into brightness./
We are sparks of starlight. /
a constellation dancing in the sky/
as we say:/

THANK YOU,/ THANK YOU VERY MUCH./

Filled with gratitude /
for every cloud, leaf and petal, /
every breath we take,/ every heartbeat,/
/we are ready, at last,/
to say what's the most important:/

I LOVE YOU, MY WORLD, /
I LOVE YOU, MY SUNLIGHT /

I give you all the love /
of my tired, grateful heart!

That's right, let's say it again./

I LOVE YOU,MY SPLENDID, STUPENDOUS, EXQUISITE,
DELIGHTFULAND MAGNIFICENT LIFE!

Now, step by step,
one word at a time...

*NOTE: Each phrase to be recited by the reader
and repeated by the listeners at the / sign.*

"Pink Infinity"

A Rainbow Vision

Light ascends from circle to circle.

The first glows like a wine-red ruby
brimming with the mysteries of life.

The second— amber— attracts, inspires
with riches of smoothly flowing honey.

The third holds it all together, outlined
in precious metal, brightly polished gold.

The fourth scatters soft rose petals
on the hard, green jade. Together,
they explode into emerald glow.

You see the fifth, the clearest sky-blue of
azure, laced with sapphire and turquoise.

The sixth, an amethyst of unseen beauty —
shines with pure violet light, from within.

The seventh— don't forget the seventh—
is the crown of a thousand petals,

sparkling with the brightness of
white diamonds, star crystals of light.

The Infinity Room

... is closed, they say, at the Broad Museum.
I do not trust them. I would not go in, anyway.

I find my own Infinity on the beach –
floating on the waves that crossed the Pacific
to lick my toes covered with sand crystals.
It is scattered among the multicolored pebbles
in shallow tide pools I walk through to reach you.

I'm home now.

My infinity stirs in dewdrops on the grass –
diamond sparks on moss green, chartreuse
and celadon shining in early spring light.

It tastes refreshing in cold juice
of an orange picked in my garden
when it's 33 outside. It echoes
in the melodious phrases
of the mockingbird, claiming the top
of my pine, its contours outlined
against the misty hilltops
and the bluest of California skies.

Where is ours? Where do you find
that spark, that voice,
that calling?

Is it the sunrays bouncing off
the mirror surface of the lake?
Splitting into a myriad prisms
dancing between your fingers?
Your private rainbow? Or when you

walk into the room
with Jeff Koontz balloons
and see yourself reflected
in the smooth, polished skins
bright and translucent
like air bubbles,
a giant child's delight?

I hold a bouquet of infinity in my hand.
It opens to blossom
in ellipses, circles, petals –
intersecting trajectories of light,
reverberations of energy
reflecting a multitude of time-lines –

crystal after crystal – wave after wave

carnelian into amber into gold –
emerald, turquoise, and sapphire –

amethyst radiance above a myriad
of cupolas – other infinities
that pass me by

Meditation on Light

Close your eyes. Take a deep breath. Relax.

Imagine a bright, golden-white light right above your head, a miniature sun. Its golden rays shine all around you, through you. You are surrounded, enveloped, protected by light. You are Light. You are Love. You are safe.

Now, breathe in this light. See how it starts to shine inside you. With each breath, the brightness descends into you, deeper and deeper. Light enters and fills you. It shines inside your head. You see it in your mind's eye. Light particles scatter and flow in waves. All your thoughts are pure light. There is no darkness. Only light, only peace.

Now, the white light expands and settles in your heart. A sun shines in the middle of your chest. It stays there. The pulsating sun-heart moves the golden-white, dazzling light into all parts of your body. Your blood and veins are full of light. A warm glow spreads all over. Darkness disappears. Light is everything.

Streams of light flow through all your organs, muscles, and skin. Light rays cleanse, purify, and heal. They flow to the fingertips, the tips of your toes, through your eyes, ears, mouth, and nose. Even your hair is full of light. From the top of your head to the soles of your feet, you are all made of light.

Breathe deeply. Breathe in— breathe out—
Breathe in— breathe out. Now—in this moment—next—

The energy flows and pulsates. You feel lighter, fuller, calmer, brighter. You are joyous, thankful. Shining with the golden-white glow of your light, you feel vibrant, fully alive.

You say YES to the light, YES to the life this light brings.

You rest in the tranquil rhythm of your breath. Rest
in the strong, steady rhythm of your heartbeat—
a pulsating, bright, golden sun.

You are light. You are love.
All made of light. All made of love.
Still— silent — serene—
The brightest sun.

*   *   *

Now, open your eyes. Feel the earth beneath your feet.
See everything around you. You are here. You have arrived.

"Be the Sky" with Matilija Poppy

Imagine a Star...

... above your head. Imagine
a bright shining star
of white golden light.
Imagine a sparkling star
with long brilliant rays
wrapping your entire body
in a cocoon of light.

Imagine you are safe
in this light like a chrysalis,
waiting to become a butterfly,
like a walnut in its shell
before it grows into a tree.

Light permeates your body.
Light flows in your veins.
Light shines in your mind.
Light pulsates in your heart.

You are liquid light.

You are light.
You are love.
You are safe.

A Declaration

I am a sovereign citizen of the galaxy.
My heart goes out to the mountains.
My feet grow roots in the light.
My eyes touchthe firmament of stars.
I breathe the gold air of goodness.
I drink the lucid water of joy.
Nourished by divine affection, I thrive,
linked to all living beings —
snow crystals, seeds, trees and sunlight.
In harmony, we sing the chorale of dawn.
I choose to love all, live in love.

I thank light for its warm brightness.
I thank trees for their fruit, for leaves
giving oxygen. For strength and patience.
I thank water for its lucid beauty
in streams, rivers, lakes and oceans
sustaining me, a parched droplet
of stardust. I thank air flowing in my lungs
and whispering in the treetops.
I thank the Universe and stars
that exploded eons ago
for the gift of my body.
I am grateful to you all.

I am a sovereign citizen of the galaxy.
My life is a song of gratitude.
I sing, I love, I sing.

Incantations

*May the blessing of light be on you
Light without and light within.
May the blessed sunlight shine on you
And warm your heart till it glows
Like a great peat fire.*

Morning Greetings

May your grace brighten my day
God of Life
God of Light
God of Love

May your kindness shine in my eyes
God of Life
God of Light
God of Love

May your joy lighten my heart
God of Life
God of Light
God of Love

Open my eyes — Open my mind — Open my heart
Let me see — Let me feel — Let me give
The gift of Love
The gift of Joy
The gift of Peace

Let me be —good, patient, and kind
Let me be —gentle, faithful, and true
Let me be —the best possible me
All morning
All evening
All night

Let me shine
With your Love and Light
All day today and my whole life

Breathing Light

for breathing in — breathing out

I am loved — I love
I am a gift — I give

I am creative — I create
I am beautiful — I share beauty

I am peaceful — I share peace
I am joyful — I share joy

I am patient — I wait in silence
I am kind — I share kindness

I am strong — I share strength
I am wise — I share wisdom

I am Love in action
I am Light shining in all

"Diamonds"

Giving and Receiving
An Alphabet Game

When I give — I receive

Affection	—	Affirmation
Blessing	—	Bliss
Caring	—	Cherishing
Devotion	—	Delight
Excellent	—	Exquisite
Friendship	—	Fun
Grace	—	Gratitude
Honor	—	Humor
Inspiration	—	Insight
Joy	—	Jewel
Kindness	—	Kinship
Love	—	Light

As you give, so you receive
The game continues, from A to Z

Blessings to blessings
joy to joy, light to light

"Into the Light, into the Lake"

Today

I am a miracle of life

I do what I want
I want what I do

I am perfect

I am a cosmic tree
I grow by the calm lake of light

Its smooth opal surface
Reflects the sun's smiling face

My roots drink liquid light
My crown sparkles with stars

My leaves are green with peace
My flowers are gold with joy
My fruit is ripe with wisdom

I am a living miracle
I am perfect

From noon to midnight
From midnight to noon

I love what I do
I do what I love

I am – I shine
I am one with One

I am perfect

On Being a Tree

I am a tree —
My roots search for water
I drink, I grow, I live

I am a tree —
My branches greet the wind
I dance, I grow, I live
I am a tree —
My bark is moist with rain
I drink, I grow, I live

I am a tree —
My leaves kiss the sun
I breathe, I grow, I live

I am a tree —
My blossoms mirror stars
I bloom, I grow, I live

I am a tree —
My fruit feeds the world
I give, I grow, I live

"A Jewel Leaf"

In the Sun

I'm in the heart of the Sun
I AM the heart of the Sun

I'm in the rays of the Sun
I AM the rays of the Sun

I'm in the Sun's corona
I AM the Sun's corona

I'm in the Solar wind
I AM the Solar wind

I'm in the stream of Light
I AM the stream of Light

I'm in the Sun's golden heart
I AM the Sun's golden heart

I'm in the Sun's brightness
I AM the Sun's brightness

I'm in the Sunlight's blaze
I AM the Sunlight's blaze

I'm in the life-giving Light
I AM the life-giving Light

Crown Jewels

I am an onyx of grounding
I am amber of attraction
I am a topaz of resilience

I am a rose quartz of affection
I am a turquoise of expression
I am an amethyst of insight

I am a sapphire of faith
I am an emerald of hope
I am a ruby of love

I am a crystal of clarity
I am a pearl of understanding
I am a diamond of light

"A Shell Full of Gemstones"

The Seven Suns

With deep breaths, I greet the sunrise.
Bright sun above my head. Its light rays all around me.
Bright sun in my mind. Bright sun in my heart.

The first sun is alive — *I live*

The red circle spins. The red sun shines.
The coral circle spins. The coral sun shines.
The ruby circle spins. The ruby sun shines.

Red — Coral — Ruby — Carnelian

I am Divine Matter
I am Divine Body
I am Divine Presence

Faster— brighter — spinning — shining —

Matter — Body — Presence

I am a Red Ruby — Alive

The second sun is aflame — *I give*

The orange circle spins. The orange sun shines.
The copper circle spins. The copper sun shines.
The amber circle spins. The amber sun shines.

I am Divine Spark
I am Divine Flame
I am Divine Intention

Orange — Jasper — Copper — Amber

Faster— brighter — spinning — shining —

Spark — Flame — Intention

I am a Pure Amber — Aflame

The third sun is ablaze — *I hold*

The yellow circle spins. The yellow sun shines.
The topaz circle spins. The topaz sun shines.
The gold circle spins. The gold sun shines.

Yellow — Gold — Topaz — Citrine

I am Divine Energy
I am Divine Balance
I am Divine Strength

Faster— brighter — spinning — shining —

Energy — Balance — Strength

I am Bright Gold — Ablaze

The fourth sun is aglow — *I love*

The green circle spins. The green sun shines.
The jade circle spins. The jade sun shines.
The emerald circle spins. The emerald sun shines.

Green — Jade — Garnet — Emerald

I am Divine Kindness
I am Divine Love
I am Divine Compassion

Faster— brighter — spinning — shining —

Kindness — Love — Compassion

I am a Green Emerald — Aglow

The fifth sun is aware — *I speak*

The blue circle spins. The blue sun shines.
The turquoise circle spins. The turquoise sun shines.
The sapphire circle spins. The sapphire sun shines.

Blue — Aquamarine — Turquoise — Sapphire

I am Divine Voice
I am Divine Expression
I am Divine Truth

Faster— brighter — spinning — shining —

Voice — Expression — Truth

I am a Blue Sapphire — Aware

The sixth sun is awake — *I see*

The violet circle spins. The violet sun shines.
The lapis circle spins. The lapis sun shines.
The amethyst circle spins. The amethyst sun shines.

Violet — Opal — Lapis Lazuli — Amethyst

I am Divine Vision
I am Divine Insight
I am Divine Wisdom

Faster— brighter — spinning — shining —

Vision — Insight — Wisdom

I am a Clear Amethyst — Awake

The seventh sun is alight — *I shine*

The white circle spins. The white sun shines.
The diamond circle spins. The diamond sun shines.
The crystal circle spins. The crystal sun shines.

White— Quartz — Diamond — Crystal

I am Divine Radiance
I am Divine Clarity
I am Divine Light

Faster — brighter — spinning — shining —

Radiance — Clarity — Light

I am a Diamond Sun — All Light

I am immersed in the Light Sphere
I am a droplet in the Light Ocean

*   *   *

The circles spin, laughing. The suns glow with joy.

Matter — Body — Presence —
Spark — Flame — Intention —
Energy — Balance — Strength —
Kindness — Love — Compassion —
Voice — Expression — Truth —
Vision — Insight — Wisdom —
Radiance — Clarity — Light —

I am a rainbow of light
I am a rainbow of love

I am all made of light
I am all made of love

I am light
I am love

I am

*   *   *

With deep breaths, I bless the sunset.

The white circle rests. The white sun sleeps.
The violet circle rests. The violet sun sleeps.
The blue circle rests. The blue sun sleeps.
The green circle rests. The green sun sleeps.
The yellow circle rests. The yellow sun sleeps.
The orange circle rests. The orange sun sleeps.
The red circle rests. The red sun sleeps.

I am Love in action
I am Light shining in all

Amen — Let it be
God's Light shines in me

Amen — Let it be
God's Love shines in me

"Steps to Perfection"

The Divine Path

I am a Spark of Cosmic Fire
I am the purity of God's heart
I am a Spark of Cosmic Fire
I am the perfection of God's mind

The Divine Mind of God and I are One
The Divine Heart of God and I are One

       I am Divine Light
       I am Divine Love
       I am Divine Faith
       I am Divine Truth
       I am Divine Spark
       I am Divine Strength
       I am Divine Presence
       I am Divine Radiance

I am Love in action
I am Light shining in all

I live in the Light of Divine Mind
I live in the Love of Divine Heart

       I am Divine Joy
       I am Divine Peace
       I am Divine Beauty
       I am Divine Grace
       I am Divine Harmony
       I am Divine Serenity
       I am Divine Gratitude
       I am Divine Abundance

I am Love in action
I am Light shining in all

For the gift of freedom
Praise God's Holy Name

For the new beginning
Thank the One, True Love

For the spring of joy
Sing the purest song

Of Love that was, is
And forever will be in you—
With you—around you

Love the Love—
Love the Greatest Love—
Praise God's Holy Name —

Amen — Let it be
God's Love shines through me

Amen — Let it be
God's Light shines through me

"Reflections"

The Stream

I am the stream of Love
I flow towards the Divine
to all, in all, through all

I am the wave of Light
I move towards the Divine
to all, in all, through all

I am the cup of Love
I'm filled with Love Divine
for all, from all, in all

I am the spark of Light
I shine with Light Divine
for all, in all, through all

I am the sea of Love
I'm filled with Love Divine
for all, from all, in all

I am the ocean of Light
I shine with Light Divine
for all, in all, through all

Blessed be the stream
Blessed be the wave

Blessed be the cup
Blessed be the spark

Blessed be the sea
Blessed be the ocean

Now and Before and After
Now and Now and Now

"Willow Lake"

The Shield of Light

I call upon God's True Light
to fill me, protect me, and guide me

> Light around me
> Light within me
> Light without

> Light before me
> Light behind me
> Light inside

> Light on my left
> Light on my right
> Light throughout

> Light above me
> Light below me
> Light in my heart

Thank you God
for the gift of your Light
Let it shine, let it be

Now and Before and After
Now and Now and Now

The Shield of Love

I call upon God's true Love
To fill me, protect me, and guide me

Love around me
Love within me
Love without

Love before me
Love behind me
Love inside

Love on my left
Love on my right
Love throughout

Love above me
Love below me
Love in my heart

Thank you, God
For the gift of your Love
Let it shine, let it be

Now and Before and After
Now and Now and Now

The End

About the Author

Maja Trochimczyk, Ph.D., is a Polish American poet, music historian, photographer, and author of six books on music, most recently *Frédéric Chopin: A Research and Information Guide* (rev. ed., 2015). Trochimczyk's seven books of poetry include *Rose Always, Miriam's Iris, Slicing the Bread, The Rainy Bread,* and two anthologies, *Chopin with Cherries* and *Meditations on Divine Names*. A former Poet Laureate of Sunland- Tujunga, she is the founder of Moonrise Press, and Board Secretary of the Polish American Historical Association. Hundreds of her poems, studies, articles and book chapters appeared in English, Polish, and in many translations. She read papers at over 80 international conferences and is a recipient of honors and awards from Polish, Canadian, and American institutions, such as the American Council of Learned Societies, the Polish Ministry of Culture, PAHA, McGill University, and the University of Southern California.

www.trochimczyk.net